ART DECO

IN THE

PHILIPPINES

ART DECO

IN THE

PHILIPPINES

Edited by

Lourdes R. Montinola

Contributing Authors

Gerard Rey Lico
Lourdes R. Montinola
Manuel Maximo Lopez del Castillo-Noche
John L. Silva
Augusto F. Villalón

For all who treasure the heritage
and history of their country

Art Deco in the Philippines
2010 © ArtPostAsia Pte Ltd

Editor
Lourdes R. Montinola

Contributing Authors
Gerard Rey Lico
Lourdes R. Montinola
Manuel Maximo Lopez del Castillo-Noche
John L. Silva
Augusto F. Villalón

Copy Editor
Lorna K. Tirol

Book and Design Development
Tina Colayco

Designer
Sergio Bumatay III

Project Managers
Jacky Arquiza
Rina Camacho

Publications Director
Melody Gocheco

Produced and Designed by
ArtPostAsia Pte Ltd
Email: publications@artpostasia.com

www.artpostasia.com

First Edition 2010

Hard Cover ISBN 978-971-0579-06-8
Soft Cover ISBN 978-971-0579-05-1

Page 1. *Sculpture by Francesco Riccardo Monti
outside the Metropolitan Theater.*
Page 2. *Sculpture of Eve by Francesco Riccardo
Monti at the lobby of the Metropolitan Theater.*
Page 4. *An architectural Art Deco stunner is the
circular rooftop glass skylight of the Far Eastern
University Administration Building, Manila.*
Pages 5. *Far Eastern University, Manila.*
This page. *Rear view elevation of the Tomas Mapua
Art Deco home.*

CONTENTS

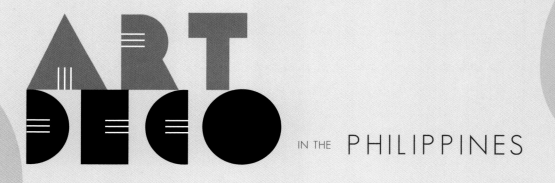

ART DECO IN THE PHILIPPINES

Lourdes R. Montinola

Less than twenty years ago, not many in Manila, even among architects and interior designers, recognized, much less appreciated the Art Deco style. I myself was introduced to it by a Benedictine monk, an architect, who invited me years ago to view outstanding specimens of Art Deco "before they disappear." True enough, we have since lost many famous houses, buildings, and cinemas, all of them in the Deco medium. Undocumented treasures may also have been destroyed in the provinces.

Today, the term *Art Deco* is much bruited about because after our architects' dalliance with the fashionable trends in architecture—the International, the California Moderne, the Philippine Colonial, the Mediterranean, the Asian—there is now an appreciation of artistic creations of less than a century ago. Art Deco tours around the city, mostly in Old Manila and even in the cemeteries, have suddenly become popular. Heritage conservationists, architects, and designers spurred the renewed interest in this decorative style that flourished between the first and second world wars.

Art Deco is derived from a 1925 exhibition in Paris called the *Exposition Internationale des Arts Décoratifs et Industriels Modernes*. The style took the world by storm and spread not only to Europe but also to America where it had the greatest impact. It drew from many inspirations—the exotic, Cubism, the Ballets Russes, Egypt, Aztec Mexico and Peru, and Africa—and encompassed not only architecture but also a wide spectrum of the applied arts. It also inspired a radical mode of dress wear, and created new jewelry, furniture, and sculpture.

The mid-1930s brought about American Deco, manifested in New York skyscrapers and by the "streamlined" look. It spread to as far as Japan, India, Australia, and Shanghai. Although the Philippines is at the farthest end of the map, its gifted architects came home from abroad and created works of art inspired by their observations but adapted to their own culture. Some of these works were their interpretations of Art Deco.

Its official reign was from 1910 to 1939, but in the Philippines it lasted into the 1940s and thereafter, in some records. Here, as in the rest of the world, cinemas and palaces of pleasure were among the buildings constructed in the Art Deco style.

In this book, a few Art Deco lovers attempt to record its presence in prominent homes and buildings in Manila, Iloilo, and Quezon. It is hoped that more excellent examples in other provinces will be identified and documented. A study of this unique and stunning style may help us to rediscover and appreciate the Art Deco treasures in our midst. In reopening our eyes to the lifestyle of only a generation ago, we may discover the genius of our own artisans or perhaps recognize their artistic creations in our own homes or surroundings. It is also hoped that the journey of discovery can lead us to conserve extant Art Deco works and fit them to adaptive use. ◎

Page 9. *Minarets of the Metropolitan Theater, Manila.*

Opposite page. *Art Deco grillwork behind glass doors and on railings at the balconies and veranda of the Administration Building, Far Eastern University, Manila.*

Right. *Art Deco grillwork on entrance door and staircase of the Mayflower Building in Singalong, Manila, which was formerly occupied by the Instituto Cervantes. The Mayflower apartment building is one of Manila's best examples of the late 1930s look called the Streamline Moderne style.*

FILIPINO MODERNE

Augusto F. Villalón

A 1925 exhibition in Paris seeded the global Art Deco style that drew inspiration from diverse precedents, taking off from sinuous flowery Art Nouveau forms, Egyptian art, and native American art, and leading to the development of Cubism, the Bauhaus, and even Russian ballet. The machine-crisp style was characterized by linear, hard-edge, and angular composition with geometrically stylized decoration.

The "Streamline Moderne," a later stylistic variation of Art Deco, is testimony to the dawn of manufacturing, of new machines and technological breakthroughs. Everything was moving forward at great speed. To achieve more of that much-desired speed, ocean liners, automobiles, and airplanes had to be streamlined. Streamlining developed into the shape that best expressed the fascination with speed; architecture, interior, and furniture design followed suit. The age of dawning consumerism dictated the same design fate for mass-produced home appliances such as refrigerators and radio. Sophisticated design was now within everyone's reach. The Art Deco style encompassed more than just architecture; in its total package was everything expressive of the vibrant energy of that era that broke old barriers and created new horizons.

Jazz moved out of New Orleans back rooms and went mainstream, and people the world over embraced it. Artists stepped out of hidden boxes and into the uncharted world of the abstract. Cocteau, Gide, and others experimented in theater. It was time for the avant-garde, for change, for reestablishing that life existed beyond the pain caused by World War I. It was time for idealism, for believing, for looking forward.

Finally out of the Spanish sphere and now firmly in the American orbit, the Philippines was looking outward, away from its island shell, and falling in step with the world. The American-established educational system produced its first graduates. The first set of scholars sent to the United States had returned home. The economy, fueled mostly by agriculture, boomed. Air travel to the United States was introduced. The footprint of Manila was changing quickly; the city was expanding. America was now promising independence. There was much to do, and even more to look forward to.

"Modernism, as it should be, is not a passing fancy," the *Sunday Tribune Magazine* observed in 1936. "It is a style which, like the Gothic or the Renaissance, shall live for quite a long time. And like the other styles that came before it, Modernism is an adequate and eloquent expression of its age. It has one credo: everything has a definite use. And to achieve this purpose, Modernism employs nothing but simple and direct lines."

Indeed, the 1930s machine-age ethic demanded simple, direct lines. Wall surfaces, whether straight or curved, were stretched drumskin-taut, like the bows of ocean liners, pierced by porthole-round windows to complete the image. Reinforced concrete, milled lumber, corrugated galvanized-iron roofing, steel sash windows, and glass were new, standardized building technology elements that made it possible to achieve that machine-like precision. Architecture was a fluid, rigidly geometric juxtaposition of volumes, planes, and straight lines.

Filipino creativity, responding to the tropical environment, softened the severe Western architectural style. Thin concrete slabs broke flat façades, protruding from unadorned wall surfaces to protect door and window openings from torrential monsoon rains and the hot sun. For increased air circulation in the hot and humid Philippine tropics, windows were enlarged and geometric hand-wrought iron grills covered openings cut into the exterior walls for ventilation. At the Far Eastern University (FEU) in Manila, the wall of translucent glass blocks so typical of 1930s Art Deco architecture features a tropical twist—instead of the expected solid wall of square glass blocks, it is a checkerboard with open and closed squares of glass blocks to allow airflow.

Top. *Detail of iron grill support of wooden railings in the Administration Building of Far Eastern University, Manila, built by Pablo Antonio.*

Above. *Grillwork and glass block detail at the Far Eastern University's Administration Building.*

Opposite page. *Detail of marbleized posts of the Tomas Mapua house on Taft Avenue Extension, Pasay City. Stylized flowers and leaves in Art Deco design.*

features a tropical twist—instead of the expected solid wall of square glass blocks, it is a checkerboard with open and closed squares of glass blocks to allow airflow.

The deep greens of tropical foliage in gardens with full-grown hardwood trees shading buildings from the sun further softened the hard, tight architectural lines. Adaptation of Filipino elements in Art Deco detailing—stylized flora, fauna, folk art patterns, and even mythological figures—infused the otherwise foreign style with a distinctly Filipino dimension. The wealth of detail surviving in Manila's Metropolitan Theater by architect Juan Arellano is testimony to the creativity and cultural grounding of the Filipino artist despite working in a Western idiom.

At first appearance, Art Deco in the Philippines follows the dictates of the international style. Upon closer inspection, however, the Filipino overlay to the style is obvious. The Filipino, a master of adaptation, has created a national version of the international Art Deco.

Moderne architecture style took the world by storm as it did the Philippines. It was the perfect vocabulary for the country to showcase the Commonwealth era's thrust to fall in step with the world and with the 20th century. Those were heady, adolescent days for the Philippines, and now a forgotten era whose golden memory this book hopes to revive. ☺

A Nationwide Heritage of Philippine ART DECO

Vito Cruz:
A former enclave of
Art Deco style in Manila

Lourdes R. Montinola

The architects who returned from studies abroad in the early 1900s, like Tomas Mapua in 1911 and Juan Arellano in 1917, started to build in the prevailing traditional and neoclassic styles but soon shifted to modernism. They introduced Art Deco in the Philippines in the late 1920s and 1930s, about the time its influence was very strong in the United States. Because Deco could be naturalized and adapted to incorporate native decorative features, the architects and designers experimented with the use of local materials.

Façade of the Hidalgo-Lim house on Vito Cruz St., Manila.

Vito Cruz Street, a new fashionable residential area just off Manila's Taft Avenue, boasted a row of houses from this period. Across was the Rizal Memorial Sports Complex built around 1934, also in the Art Deco style. Most of the houses were owned by affluent families from the Philippine provinces of Iloilo and Negros, others by prominent Manila families. There were originally nine homes done in the Art Deco style, mostly three-story mansions, but some of them were destroyed during World War II. Among those that were spared was the house of Gen. Vicente Lim and his wife, Pilar Hidalgo. Their daughter Eulalia restored it in 1994, and I was privileged to visit it then.

Entrance gate of the Hidalgo-Lim house at #616 Vito Cruz St., Manila.

The house was designed and built in 1930 by Juan Nakpil, who had just arrived from studies at the École de Beaux-Arts in Paris. He had been influenced by homes he had seen abroad, but he wanted to create something Philippine. The tropical climate called for the features of the traditional Philippine *bahay na bato* (stone house)—high ceilings and cross ventilation.

Entrance to the Hidalgo-Lim house through a narrow covered porch facing Vito Cruz St., Manila. The grillwork of the ground floor windows and doors and the railings in front of the upstairs bedroom were all designed by Juan Nakpil.

I was impressed by the woodwork as I entered the house. The walls, posts, cornices, and geometrically arched partitions—made of *narra* hardwood in a beautiful walnut color—were linear in detail, a departure from the lacy *calado* (fretwork) and curves, particularly of the Art Nouveau-influenced houses of the past. The floors—of hardy *ipil* from Palawan—were fitted; no nails were evident on the surface as the planks had been grooved and the nails placed on the underside.

An outstanding feature of the house was the floor-to-ceiling window effect with graceful grillwork, more curving than linear, but much simpler than the intricate floral styles of the previous periods. Cross ventilation was provided by large windows that jutted out of the window sills. Below the window sills were sliding doors that opened to more grills, taking inspiration from the *ventanillas* of the old colonial homes which effectively provided for the additional flow of air from floor to ceiling, and gave a wider view of the gardens as well. The grills were especially designed by Nakpil.

Left. *Grillwork on the second floor balcony, with its arched windows and doors of the Hidalgo-Lim house on Vito Cruz St., Manila.*

Opposite page. *Found inside the Hidalgo-Lim house are floor-to-ceiling windows with* ventanillas *below sills for air circulation. At the entrance of the dining room are geometric designs in wood detail.*

Translucent *capiz* shells were used like glass to filter in sunlight from transoms on top of doors that led to the terrace. This was a Philippine touch, as were the decorative octagonal *capiz* shell ornaments with painted red flowers that hung on the walls. Elegant beveled and etched glass protected by decorative grills on the big doors also brought in light from the outside.

On the ground floor, the living room flowed into the dining room, whose walls were painted with jungle birds and tropical plants. The stairway leading to the second floor was lighted by stained-glass

Left. *Beveled and etched glass door with translucent* capiz *shell transoms lead out to the garden in the Hidalgo-Lim house on Vito Cruz St., Manila.*

Opposite page. *Dining room walls painted with jungle birds and tropical plants of the Hidalgo-Lim house.*

A stained-glass window depicting Art Deco motifs provides sunlight to the staircase leading up to the second floor of the Hidalgo-Lim house on Vito Cruz St., Manila. The window was made by Matthias Kraut, a German who brought the craft to the Philippines.

windows made by Matthias Kraut, a German who had brought the craft to the Philippines. Upstairs were three enormous bedrooms.

Juan Nakpil also built Art Deco mansions on Vito Cruz for the families of Ricardo Lacson and Manuel Javellana. These were burned by the Japanese during the liberation of Manila in 1945. Also partially burned was the house of Justice and Mrs. Antonio Villareal that was designed by Pablo Antonio. Fortunately, it was restored and successfully remodeled into a boutique hotel. Nakpil and Antonio would build more outstanding Art Deco homes in the neighboring areas, and eventually become National Artists for Architecture.

The last house on the street was built in 1936 by Juan Arellano, the architect of the Metropolitan Theater, for Federico Benedicto Montinola and his wife Espectacion Lopez Ledesma. It was spared from the war and continues to be used by the Montinola heirs. The other homes—of the Alejandro Roceses, Filomena Legardas, Perez

The Manuel Javellana house on Vito Cruz St., Manila built in 1938.

Rubios, Chancos, Enriquezes, and Javellanas—changed hands after being restored. The Lacson home, together with the adjacent Legarda property, has been converted into a Buddhist temple.

Vito Cruz also attracted embassies and consulates—Russian, French, Indonesian, and Vietnamese, of which only the last remains.

Real estate developers now continue to eye the whole Vito Cruz area for conversion into a commercial center with shopping malls and high-rise apartments. Fortunately, the three families left that continue to own their Vito Cruz homes are determined to preserve the heritage of their home and their family. ⊚

The Ricardo Lacson house on Vito Cruz St., Manila, built in the 1930s.

Left. *Justice and Mrs. Antonio Villareal's house on Vito Cruz St., Manila in the 1930s. This home was remodeled to a boutique hotel (refer to pages 28-29).*

Below, left and right. *Art Deco grillwork on the staircase railing of the Villareal house.*

This page and opposite. *The Orchid Garden Hotel, the former home of Justice and Mrs. Antonio Villareal on Vito Cruz St., Manila.*

This page. *Mr. and Mrs. Federico Montinola's house on Vito Cruz St., Manila, built in the 1930s.*

Above. *Floor of vestibule with Italian cutout marble designed by an Italian artist. Beyond is the well-ventilated dining room of the Montinola house.*

Left. *Entrance doors to the Montinola house with Art Deco detail on the lintel.*

The Tomas Mapua House

Lourdes R. Montinola

Amazing, but true. If one could find in London in 1929 an Art Deco house that was furnished by famous Art Deco designers, in Manila two years later there was such a house as well, but utilizing Philippine materials and incorporating Philippine architectural features that made it suitable to the tropics.

This Filipino house was an example of Art Deco at its best. It was designed and built for his family by Tomas Mapua, a Cornell graduate and the Philippines' first registered architect. He designed the furniture and conceived all the decorative details, giving his home an integrated look.

Tomas Mapua house built in 1931 on Taft Avenue Extension, Pasay City.

Opposite page. *(top) Blueprint drawing of the Mapua house south elevation; (bottom) drawing of the front view of the home.*

Mapua built the house on a 3,000-square-meter lot on Taft Avenue Extension in Pasay City. Miraculously spared from destruction during the liberation of Manila from the Japanese in 1945, it is still home to the family of the late Roberto and Gloria (Mapua) Lim.

The house makes a statement right at its gate. The grillwork on the imposing gate and fence is typically geometric, using straight lines and triangles. The light fixtures built into the posts have a simple, elongated design as well.

This is a house that brings the outdoors in. The magnificent high-ceilinged *sala* (living room) opens out to porches with French doors,

Top. *Mr. and Mrs. Tomas Mapua*

Above. *An early photo of the Tomas Mapua house on Taft Avenue Extension, Pasay City.*

Right. *Entrance gate to the Tomas Mapua house with geometric design on grillwork and lamp posts.*

and the bedrooms to balconies. The house must have defied the rules of security then, but it demonstrated the new emphasis on space, ventilation, and light.

The ceiling is a work of art, displaying a mural of a mythical figure, with Chinese stylized clouds mostly in gold, bordered by a wide band of *capiz* shell that serves as a light diffuser while adding a touch of Philippine tropical design. Bordering the *capiz* are a cornice and an intricately carved frieze.

Emphasized in the house are the geometric lines echoed in the boxy, simple furniture and enhanced by stylized floral carving. Philippine wood is highlighted in both the furniture and the geometrically designed parquet floor. The furniture is mostly dark, decorated

This page. *Ceiling mural in the Tomas Mapua living room with a rainbow, Chinese stylized clouds, and birds bordered by a wide band of* capiz *shell light diffusers, and a cornice with an intricately carved frieze.*

In the Tomas Mapua house, the living room opens out to the porch and gardens through steel-framed glass doors. The furniture is enhanced by stylized floral or geometrical carvings. A wood cabinet with carved door panels in a light color stands in contrast to mostly dark furniture.

with contrasting carved panels in lighter wood. The designs on the carvings are mainly floral or geometrical.

Two built-in alcoves in the dining room house porcelain and other collections, typical of the Art Deco homes in Europe. The dining set, buffet and chairs are elegantly modern—the table chamfered off at the four corners, and the broad table supports enhanced with carvings of foliage. The kitchen doors have the typical stylized bouquet, and most of the carvings are of the stylized rose, an Art Deco icon famously known as the French or Iribe rose.

Notable in the dining room chairs is the use of *bijuco* (rattan) or *solihiya* (cane) for the seats, another trick for achieving coolness through air circulation, and contributing to the native look. Most authentic is the lighting fixture—a very simple, modern geometrical opaque-glass version, providing the indirect lighting in vogue at the time.

Above. *The dining room of the Tomas Mapua house was decorated with chairs of* bijuco *(rattan) and* solihiya *(cane). The pantry doors and buffet side table are carved with details of stylized fruits and flowers. A geometrical opaque glass lighting fixture hangs from the ceiling.*

Right. *The modern table in the dining room chamfered off at the four corners and enhanced with foliage carvings.*

This page. *The doors leading into the kitchen of the Tomas Mapua house have the period's typical stylized decoration.*

Opposite page. *A boxy set of chairs with cane seats at the Tomas Mapua house. Behind are doors leading to a balcony that looks out to the garden. A variety of Philippine hardwoods was used for flooring in the home.*

Far Left. *Art Deco grillwork on the window looking out to the garden.*

Left. *Floral detail on the table leg. (refer to page 40)*

Below. *Detail of the service staircase. A bell to summon the help can be rung from an upper floor.*

As in the Metropolitan Theater in Manila, the base of the staircase handrails is a stunning piece of sculpture—dark wood embellished at the top by carved, stylized flowers in a lighter veneer. Stained-glass windows brighten this staircase.

Truly, as Gina Mapua Lim, herself an artist, observes, Philippine craftsmanship in architecture peaked at the time houses like theirs were built. ⊚

Opposite page. *The Tomas Mapua staircase to the upstairs bedrooms decorated with stained-glass windows and a lighting fixture of interlocking sheets of frosted glass, which was designed by Mapua himself.*

Below. *Newel post of solid hardwood capped by gilded Art Deco incisions.*

Our Iloilo Boathouse

John L. Silva

Above. *A side view of the Ledesma Boathouse. To the left are the upper and lower balconies facing the Iloilo River. Note the windows flushed to the corner. c. 1954.*

Opposite page. *The Boathouse of Julio Ledesma, designed by Juan Nakpil and built c. 1937 on General Luna Street in Iloilo City. The house was a present for his son Juan Ledesma and his wife Magdalena Javellana Ledesma. The house was in the "Streamline Moderne" mode of Art Deco. The author is the great-grandson of Julio Ledesma.*

In 1936, my great-grandfather, Julio Ledesma, took his family on a voyage around the world. Art Deco by then was over ten years old and its design influences ran the gamut from jewelry to cruise-liner interiors to cars and all the way to skyscrapers.

In the United States, the family visited newly built Deco landmarks such as the Rockefeller Center and the Golden Gate Bridge, and stayed in fancy hotels with Deco furnishings. On a liner on their return to the Philippines, they were surrounded by portholes, curved railings, and geometric mural patterns in the dining room and hallways, and dined on Deco-style cutlery.

By the time he returned to Iloilo, Lolo Julio knew the style of the house he would build for his son Juanito and his wife, Magdalena Javellana Ledesma, my grandparents. The house would be a homage to Art Deco.

Art Deco had various architectural strains, one being called "Streamline Moderne." Buildings of this style had less ceiling space and no Grecian columns, and the predominant lines were horizontal. Chrome or polished railings usually encircled them; the corners were rounded, as if to blend smoothly with the flow of air. There were portholes on the sides or by the entrance, and the sheen was smooth concrete painted off-white. The buildings looked poised to move, perhaps to fly.

Above left. *Hanging ceiling lamp in the lower balcony of the Ledesma Boathouse in Iloilo.*

Left. *The author, cousin Greg Lacson, and sister Marie S. Vallejo with the Boathouse behind. c. 1954.*

Right. *Porthole window at the entrance of the Ledesma Boathouse.*

Our all-white house was on General Luna Street while across the river, on E. Lopez Street, was where the Don Eugenio Lopez family would also build their own Art Deco home. (Iloilo locals, who found the two houses odd, affectionately called them "Boathouses.") Ours was built around 1936 and must have been one of Juan Nakpil's earliest works. It was a three-story cement structure, each floor encircled by an overhang band that acted as a canopy. The large gridded windows on each floor defied symmetry; they wrapped around the corners of the house, reminiscent of windows in the German Bauhaus style.

Above left and right. *Spiral staircase with Art Deco theme on banister and steps of the Lopez Boathouse in Iloilo.*

Left. *Interior of first floor landing of the Lopez Boathouse, built for Don Eugenio Lopez by Fernando Ocampo and later restored by his son, Fernando Ocampo Jr.*

The ground floor stretched from the street side all the way to the back fronting the Iloilo River. A third of the back was a concave patio open on the sides but with a ceiling. Its granite floors had colorful geometric designs, another Deco detail. A large, clear globe lamp dangled from the ceiling, and globe-like sconces were set on the outer sides of the house. Their simple industrial design resembled the flashing lights on the side of a ship's bridge or the wingtips of airplanes.

The second floor had three bedrooms, the largest of which was the master bedroom with an open-air balcony that followed the oval pattern of the patio directly underneath it.

The third floor, which was reached through an outdoor stairway attached to the wall with chrome railings, was an open-air but roofed balcony facing the street, with a large family room facing the river.

The house was confiscated during the Japanese occupation, and much of the custom-made Deco-style furniture was either destroyed, ransacked, or stolen when the Japanese surrendered. But the house itself was intact. It was eventually sold and is now a restaurant. I drop by on my visits to Iloilo, order a glass of wine in the rear patio, gaze at the river, and wistfully recall my childhood. ☺

Opposite page, top. *Rear patio of the Ledesma Boathouse.*

Opposite page, bottom. *Detail of geometrically designed balcony floor of the Ledesma Boathouse.*

Below. *An outdoor staircase leads to the third floor of the Ledesma Boathouse.*

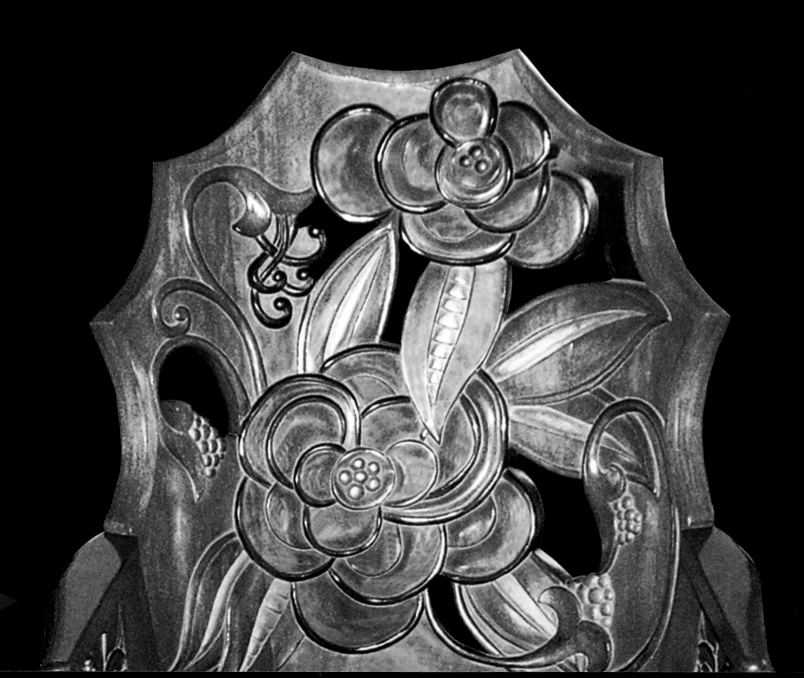

The Spirit of Sariaya, Quezon

Augusto F. Villalón

Its picturesque setting is almost perfect. The town of Sariaya (population 130,000 [National Statistics Office, 2007]) in Quezon province nests on slopes that descend gradually from mystical Mount Banahaw to the sea far beyond it. Fertile volcanic soil keeps the landscape a perennial green. A dense canopy of coconut palms stretches as far as the eye can see, owing to the town's location in one of the country's primary coconut-producing regions. Local land-owning families responded to the agriculture boom during the Philippine Commonwealth era, carving out vast plantations to cash in on the high demand for coconut oil.

Sariaya's geography gives it a special identity that distinguishes it from other towns. Its grid of streets, radiating from a central plaza, offers distant views of the natural setting—at the horizon on the uphill slope of the straight streets looms Mount Banahaw, at the end of the downhill slope is a distant view of the sea. Large Art Deco houses along

Above. *Wrought iron grillwork on the balcony of the Natalio Enriquez House (later Marquez House) in Sariaya, Quezon.*

Opposite page. *Hand-carved wooden chair with local flora—reinterpreted in geometric forms—make up the unique vocabulary Philippine Art Deco. From the Natalio Enriquez House.*

Above. *An Art Deco masterpiece is the Natalio Enriquez House (later Marquez House) in Sariaya demonstrating masterful adaptation of the Art Deco style to suit local climate, materials, and lifestyle by French-trained Architect Andres Luna de San Pedro.*

Opposite page. *So sinuous is the form of this iron-framed glass awning that serves as protection from the rain.*

the streets frame the distant natural views, create a lively streetscape, and give the town its distinct visual identity, its spirit of place. The visual harmony is enhanced by the fact that many of the houses were constructed along variations of the Art Deco style at the height of the coconut-farming industry in the 1930s.

Another factor makes Sariaya special: its Art Deco architecture takes its cues from verdant nature all around the town. Unlike the machine-sharp surfaces of the Art Deco of the era, naïf Sariaya Deco is fluid, graceful, and gracious, an architectural representation of the languid local lifestyle. Gone is the tooled precision of purist Art Deco architecture.

This is Deco of high craftsman precision, where floors carry intricate designs of inlaid Philippine hardwood, doors are carved with stylized local flora, grillwork hand-forged in the old Spanish colonial tradition has been adapted into geometric lines, and embossed relief work embellishes concrete façades with a profusion of rigidly "modern" tropical leaves.

In provincial Sariaya Art Deco, the ties with vernacular architecture remain strong. Although the architectural style is new, local building traditions are maintained. It is hybrid architecture, adapted from the West in the best Filipino tradition that stretches back to the time when vernacular architecture adapted Spanish and Chinese influences, resulting in the *bahay na bato* (stone house).

Art Deco in the West was an intellectual style with a fairly rigid vocabulary of forms; in contrast, Sariaya Deco cuts loose. It is elegant, functional, and ultramodern. Its opulence and lavishness reflect the wealth brought by agricultural bounty, its rich and festive character fitted to the cycle of traditional religious and harvest celebrations throughout the year. It is architecture totally rooted in its immediate surroundings, perfectly suited to the local culture, environment, and building technology.

Gone, too, are the Western logic and rigidity of Art Deco; this is a personal, individualistic approach to Art Deco made relevant to the planter's lifestyle in a vast Southern Luzon coconut *hacienda*. It is Philippine architecture at its delightful best. ◎

Opposite and this page. *Also French-trained, National Artist for Architecture Juan Nakpil surrounds a peacock-shaped stained-glass window with a luxurious relief of abstracted Sariaya flora.*

Public Buildings

and

STRUCTURES

Far Eastern University Campus:
Manila's outstanding urban Art Deco ensemble

Augusto F. Villalón

Young Filipinos in the 1930s were enamored with American culture and the new technology. The architectural expression was Art Deco—geometric, streamlined, the ultimate in modernity—and the new building technology was anchored on concrete and steel and suited to the Philippines' tropical climate. This was the architectural vocabulary of the Far Eastern University (FEU) campus that Pablo Antonio designed in 1939. Conceived as a modern, futuristic building, it reflected the forward vision of the Philippines and the university. Today, it is one of Manila's architectural icons and recognized in 2005 with a UNESCO Asia-Pacific Cultural Heritage Award.

Above. *The beautifully greened entrance to the Far Eastern University.*

Opposite page. *Graphic drawing of the first Far Eastern University built in 1934 in the Art Deco style on Azcarraga St., Manila. This building was demolished to give way to the new Quezon Boulevard. A replica (facing Quezon Blvd.) was built in 1939.*

Above left. *Far Eastern University, Manila shown newly built. c. 1939*

Above Right. *A postcard of Far Eastern University in the 1930s.*

Antonio established the FEU architectural image with a long, low-slung façade along Quezon Boulevard, Manila. *The Far Eastern Review*[1] described the campus as "of moderne architecture type, adapted to Philippine climatic conditions." A set of large piers anchor each end of the three-story façade that's lifted off street level by a covered arcade on the sidewalk. Capped by inverted-pyramid capitals, horizontally striated columns float the heavy building mass off the ground. The columns are a key element in the design. Beginning their rhythmic ascent at the arcade level, they continue upward, dividing the main façade into horizontal bays framed by deep piers that shade the windows between them. For protection from sun and rain, a thin band of concrete slips out a short distance away from beneath the parapet and runs across the entire façade.

The architectural façade of the Main Building (now Nicanor Reyes Hall), arranged in a series of setbacks emphasizing its geometric forms, is a hallmark of classic Philippine Art Deco.

Façade of Far Eastern University in the bustling city of Manila, 2010.

Opposite and this page. *Rigid horizontal lines on the posts in the covered sidewalk outside Far Eastern University's Nicanor Reyes Hall. The lines ground the ceiling that seems to float weightlessly over the space.*

Its rear façade has large openings that expose the interior of the U-shaped building to the central campus quadrangle. Openness is a characteristic of Antonio's architecture and essential "for the cross ventilation so necessary in the tropics[2]." A large ground-floor entrance hall once connected the covered sidewalk along Quezon Boulevard directly to the quadrangle at the rear, with foliage visible through layers of grilled doors and windows allowing natural cross ventilation. Tropical-themed iron grills separate interior workspaces, support stair railings, and reappear in the interior doorways, unifying the interior with a single, transparent visual element.

The rear façade of the Far Eastern University Nicanor Reyes Hall, where greenery softens the campus architecture.

This page. *Geometric lines counterpoint in the architectural composition of horizontals and diagonals seen in this entrance to Far Eastern University.*

This page. *The Art Deco columns inside the Administration Building of Far Eastern University are painted with the university's colors.*

Opposite page. *Bas-relief in the Administration Building by Francesco Riccardo Monti depicting the American Regime in the Philippines.*

The outdoor stairs connecting a second-level walkway to the ground are an Art Deco tour de force. Layers of thin concrete slabs swirl in gentle waves above and behind the open stairs in flowing counterpoint to the strict geometry of their floating concrete handrail. The detailing of the stairs is exquisite. Pablo Antonio Jr., himself an architect, says, "My father paid attention to detail. He would always tell us that the details are the soul of a building—how the moldings and the railings are done, how the details of a ceiling would make a difference in any structure. In fact, his clients liked him for these small details.[3]"

Above. *The geometry of horizontals and verticals impact as a strong Art Deco composition in this exterior stair of Far Eastern University.*

Below left. *A masterpiece is the sinuous concrete canopy hovering over floating stair handrails, Art Deco in motion.*

Below right. *Another version of FEU's architect, Pablo Antonio's floating handrails.*

*Today, abundant greenery around the
Far Eastern University campus contributes
to the beauty of the tropical Art Deco motif.*

The FEU Administration Building, constructed about a decade later and also designed by Antonio, closes the opposite end of the campus quadrangle. Its façade is punctuated with geometric architectural details, horizontal windows, and a balcony that opens out into a second-level viewing deck, from which university officials can watch activities at the quadrangle.

F.E.U. GIRL'S HIGH   MANILA

Left. *The Girls' High School building in Far Eastern University's earlier days.*

Below. *The Girls' High School building is now surrounded with newer buildings that blend seamlessly with older ones.*

Opposite page, top. *A tropical variation to the Art Deco style is the use of concrete canopies over windows and openings to protect the building interior from hot sun or rain, like those of the Administration Building.*

Opposite page, bottom. *The balconies of the Administration Building show intricate Art Deco grillwork on the railing and doors.*

69

This page and opposite. *The Far Eastern University campus is an urban oasis in chaotic Manila.*

The most outstanding portion of the Administration Building is the FEU Theater, its interior a swirl of green and gold, a constellation of stars illuminating the space, and stylized tracery on its walls spelling out FEU. A Deco stunner is the circular rooftop glass skylight where concentric rings of glass overlap to allow air circulation while keeping rain out. Beneath the skylight, the floor laid out in alternating light and dark *narra* (Philippine mahogany) hardwood leads the eye to a circular shaft that reaches down to light up offices and classrooms on the lower levels of the building.

Above. *Stylized tracery on the Far Eastern University Theater walls spell out FEU.*

Right. *An architectural Art Deco stunner is the circular rooftop glass skylight of the original social hall in the Administration Building.*

Opposite page. *Under a star-studded ceiling, swirling walls lead all eyes towards the Far Eastern University Theater stage. Once Manila's grandest and most technically advanced theater, the theater has been totally refurbished to recapture its former grandeur.*

The campus boasts masterworks of Philippine art, most of them from the Art Deco era. The Antonio Gonzales Dumlao mural in the Administration Building conveys the university mission. At the quadrangle, the focal point is a group of Vicente Manansala copper-sheet sculptures from the late 1960s depicting the professional disciplines offered by the university. Inside the chapel hang murals by National Artist Carlos "Botong" Francisco.

Below. *Far Eastern University chapel exterior with a specially made tile mural of Our Lady of Fatima by Vicente Manansala.*

Opposite page. *The quadrangle features four clusters of copper-sheet sculptures by Vicente Manansala.*

Left. *The tablets of the 10 Commandments represent the love of God, while the Far Eastern University seal, abacus, and skull are metaphors for the value of learning. By Vicente Manansala, in copper sheet.*

Above. *This sculpture of the historic warrior Lapu-Lapu stands for the love of country. By Vicente Manansala, in copper sheet.*

Above. *Madonna and child, the tao and his rooster. By Vicente Manansala, in copper sheet.*

Right. *This group of figures symbolizes the four freedoms: freedom from hunger, freedom from fear, freedom of speech, freedom of worship. By Vicente Manansala, in copper sheet.*

These three stained-glass panels—called *Sarimanok* (above), *Tail* (right), *and Prow* (opposite page)—*by Antonio Dumlao are inspired by Islamic design motifs of Filipinos from small Western Mindanao and Sulu Archipelago. Dumlao used a blend of inspirations of Art Deco and Cubistic fragmentation of form. These pieces, located at the Far Eastern University Administration Building, were made from glass sourced from colored soft drink, medicine, and condiment bottles.*

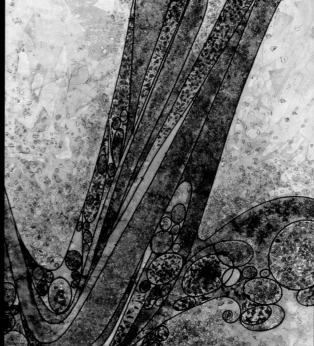

The FEU campus is one of the few ensembles in the city that exhibit architectural and stylistic integrity. It stands out amid the confusion that has befallen the University Belt (a cluster of universities and colleges in Manila). To fatigued Manila, it is a rare and shining example of respect for nature and architectural tradition. ◎

Opposite page. *A detail of the Antonio Dumlao mural in the Administration Building. The mural conveys the university mission of training the youth for progress.*

Above. *Inside the chapel are murals of the 14 Stations of the Cross by National Artist Carlos "Botong" Francisco that span both sides of the chapel walls.*

[1] "The New Far Eastern University" *The Far Eastern Review*. May 1941.
[2] Montinola, Lourdes R. *Breaking the Silence*. Diliman: University of the Philippines Press, 1996.
[3] de la Torre, Visitacion R. *The National Artists Folio 1976*. Manila: Cultural Center of the Philippines, 1976.

Metropolitan Theatre
FACADE—*Fachada*

The Metropolitan Theater

Lourdes R. Montinola

The Metropolitan Theater at the Mehan Gardens in Manila is probably the most outstanding Art Deco building in the country. Inaugurated on December 10, 1931, it was designed by the brilliant architect Juan Arellano. A.V. Hartendorp, editor of the *Philippine Education Magazine* (1932), described the theater as "modern expressionistic" and called it "the most magnificent and impressive structure ever erected in the Philippines." Fr. Bernardo Perez, an architect and Benedictine monk, referred to it as one of Arellano's romantic works, "a monumental masterpiece by a gifted architect."

Opposite page. *Metropolitan Theater blueprint.*

Right. *One of several sculptures by Francesco Riccardo Monti at the exterior of the Metropolitan Theater.*

Right and opposite page. *Stained-glass window on the theater façade with the name "Metropolitan."*

Right. *Female statues stand guard at the side entrance of the theater.*

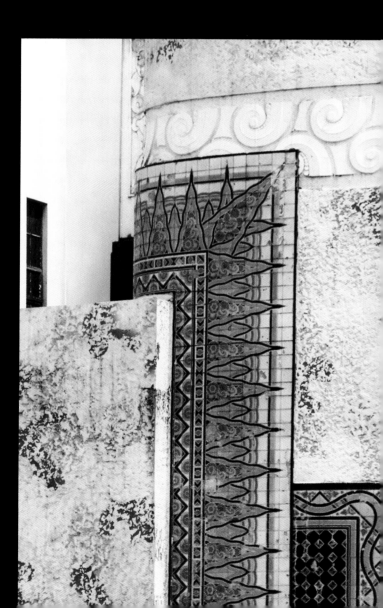

This page. *Brilliantly colored batik patterns on both sides of the Metropolitan Theater façade.*

Opposite page. *Clusters of mangoes and bananas decorate the auditorium ceiling—designed by craftsman Arcadio Arellano, brother of Juan Arellano, the theater's architect. (refer to page 88 for detailed image)*

This page. *Detail of mango and banana motifs on the Metropolitan Theater auditorium ceiling.*

In an interview in January 1930, the architect discussed his concept for this great project:

> *"The Philippines needed a modern cultural center for operas, concerts, and plays, and he planned to achieve a* monumental *one through its dimensions, elevation, and splendid decorations, and through its harmonious lines it would symbolize an organ or a cathedral."* ("El Teatro Metropolitano", Excelsior magazine, January 1930.)

He said he chose to develop something modern because first, it was a more economical method of construction, and second, it offered the opportunity to use purely native ornamentation and varied stylized forms of splendid Philippine flora, a tendency he had observed in ancient Filipino art.

A grand stained-glass window on the building façade would carry the name "Metropolitan" and bring sunlight into the lobby. The two sides flanking the main body of the façade would be like two enormous wings serving as background to the whole, and with symbols of music, pipes, or the canons of a giant organ.

The ornamentation on the walls of the inner auditorium would be sober, but the series of gradually lowered arches on the ceiling would be of rich and fragrant Philippine wood, embellished with panels bearing motifs in brilliant tones.

Arellano was especially proud of the design of the crystal lamps in the hall—bamboo stalks from whose nodes would shine the light from above and below. It was the first such design in the country. (Indirect lighting, a feature of Art Deco, was new at the time.)

Gradually lowered arches on the ceiling of the Metropolitan Theater auditorium.

The theater, when completed, proved to be an Art Deco masterpiece with impeccable acoustics and faultless lighting. With a seating capacity of 1,670, it became the venue for operas, symphony concerts, and plays for more than a decade. *Zarzuelas*, Filipino operas, films, and stage shows were also held here during the Japanese occupation of Manila.

The theater was destroyed during World War II, and for more than three decades afterward, its ruins housed a boxing arena, cheap motels and gay bars, a basketball court, and squatter families. Upon the initiative of then-Metro Manila governor Imelda Marcos, it was restored in 1978 by the architect's nephew, Otilio Arellano. It enjoyed a brief reign again as a cultural center, and finally closed down in 1996.

Opposite page, top left and right. *Archival photos of Metropolitan Theater. c. 1930s.*

Opposite page, bottom. *Metropolitan Theater façade, 1996.*

Above. *Abandoned Metropolitan Theater ballroom, 2008.*

Left. *A gathering in the ballroom of the Metropolitan Theater on the occasion of Philippine Night given by the Filipino Bluejackets of the U.S.S. Henderson, 1934.*

This first-time visitor to the theater was immediately struck by its unusual façade. The colors of the stained-glass window provided a good introduction to the exuberance that characterized the exterior. The front, according to Father Perez, was:

> "...crowned by a wall gently curved at the top, against which rose a series of pinnacles (interpreted as Muslim minarets by others). The entrance resembled a proscenium. On the lower half were doors with iron grills depicting stylized birds of paradise, and on the upper half was a large window of colored glass. The exterior proscenium was set against undulating walls decorated with brilliantly colored batik patterns." ("Major Works" Philippine Architecture II, CCP Encyclopedia of Philippine Art Volume 3. Manila: Cultural Center of the Philippines, 1994.)

At the central lobby were sculptures of Adam and Eve by the Italian sculptor Francesco Riccardo Monti. At each end of the long balcony overlooking the entrance were Fernando Amorsolo's murals *The Dance* and *The History of Music*. The grillwork on the small balconies looking out into the foyer was exceptionally elegant transitions from

Opposite page. *Iron grills at the entrance of the Metropolitan Theater.*

Above left and right. *The theater's undulating walls decorated with batik motifs and patterned tiles.*

Below. *Detail of minarets on top of the theater building.*

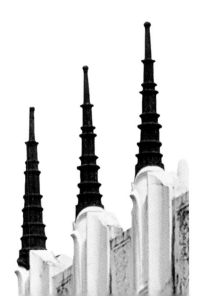

93

Art Nouveau to Art Deco. The two black posts at the bottom of the staircases were decorated with glass mosaic tiles—themselves modern pieces of sculpture in the Art Deco idiom.

The interior of the auditorium contained a wealth of decorative details. Above the proscenium were bas-relief figures emblematic of Music, Tragedy, Comedy, and Poetry. Unusual were the tall, tapering lamps of translucent glass in the form of bamboo stalks on the sides of the walls. Painted on the ceiling was a cornucopia of mangoes, bananas, and foliage designed by Juan Arellano's brother, Arcadio. This was the Philippine style of ornamentation the architect had planned.

Opposite page. *Sculptures of Adam (right) and Eve (left) by Francesco Riccardo Monti at the Metropolitan Theater central lobby.*

Above. *Grillwork on staircase railing overlooking the foyer and over the ladies' powder room.*

Left. *Black posts at the bottom of staircases decorated with glass mosaic tiles.*

This page and opposite. *Reproductions of Fernando Amorsolo's murals* The Dance *and* The History of Music *at the Metropolitan Theater lobby.*

Above. *View of the Metropolitan Theater stage, where many zarzuelas, Filipino operas, films, and stage shows were held.*

Opposite page. *Interesting lighting fixtures found throughout the Metropolitan Theater.*

Today, the Metropolitan Theater continues to struggle for existence, a victim of scant public appreciation of our talented architects' outstanding works and the lack of historical consciousness and aesthetic sense of some. However, a tripartite agreement between the Government Service Insurance System, the Manila City Hall, and the National Commission for Culture and the Arts, offers hope of a revival. Plans for a "people's theater" may yet materialize. ⑤

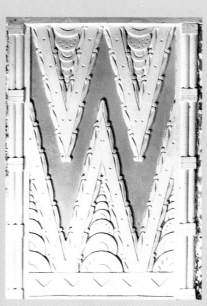

Opposite page, top. *The proscenium bas-relief figures emblematic of Tragedy, Comedy, and Poetry.*

Opposite page, bottom and this page. *Bas-relief decorations on side wall of theater.*

Above. *Detail of Metropolitan Theater interior court.*

Right. *Second floor of the Metropolitan Theater lobby.*

Opposite page. *Detail of grillwork at side entrance of the theater.*

Bayanihan Hotel and Commercial Building,
Shanom Road corner Otek Street, Baguio City,
Province of Benguet

Built in the 1950s, the Bayanihan Hotel and Commercial
Building merges ideas from the more streamlined tenets
of the International Style while adhering to Art Deco.
Decorative articulation is restricted to the play of light
and shade, particularly along the corners of the building
where vertical piers topped by protruding roundels
provide interest. The cambered edges are treated with
a combination of slender round pillars integrated with
rusticated piers and undulating porticos.

The Art Deco of Commercial Architecture

Manuel Maximo Lopez del Castillo-Noche

The commercial building sector wholeheartedly embraced Art Deco, but its various types differed in their manner of rendition, translation, and execution. They adopted the idea of not just providing space but, more significantly, uplifting people's perception of space through architecture that was inspiring, imaginative, and honestly modern.

In the country's prime commercial addresses, such as Escolta, Rosario, and Juan Luna streets in the Binondo-Santa Cruz districts of Manila, Iznart and Basa in Iloilo, Session Road in Baguio, architects articulated the features of Art Deco. Using flat, concrete planes, they employed a bevy of tricks to stylize the plasticity of concrete, thus creating fluidity, movement, and clean lines. An enhanced decorative portal,

Pablo Dulalia Building, Calle Iznart, Iloilo City, Province of Iloilo (refer to page 106 for further details)

Left. *Pablo Dulalia Building,*
Calle Iznart, Iloilo City,
Province of Iloilo

Designed by Juan Arellano in 1932,
the building carries his signature
bas-reliefs rendered in a playful
arrangement of geometric shapes,
zigzag patterns and vertical folds,
as well as stylized floral patterns that
serve as brackets for the soffits of
the arcades. Like most commercial
buildings in Iloilo City, it has not
weathered time and the elements well.

Left and Right. *Manila Electric Railroad*
and Light Company (MERALCO),
Calle San Marcelino, Ermita, Manila

The original headquarters of
MERALCO, it not only housed the
company's administrative offices but
was also the station terminus for the
tranvias *that plied the busy streets of*
Manila before World War II. Interesting
bas-reliefs grace the left corner of the
structure—eleven muses caught in a
maelstrom, furies reaching out to land,
water, and air. Unfortunately, both the
architect and the artist are unknown.

This page. *Vi-Car Building,
Calle Fernandez, Dagupan City, Province of Pangasinan*

*Built in 1950 by an unknown architect, it was once
Dagupan's popular residential and commercial structure
and today is one of its few remaining Art Deco edifices.
This imposing and elegant building has interesting
features in its upper levels. The Art Deco pediment
contains the name of the structure flanked by slender
pilotis columns supporting an undulating concrete slab.
A square piercing adorns the central vertical bay.*

usually the sole articulated feature of the structure, was decorated with the most expensive building stone available in the market, the most flamboyant grillwork, and the most technologically advanced automatic doors, lighting, and wind curtains available. Further enhancements would utilize plastered or terra cotta reliefs in strategic areas of the building, or would traverse, like a ribbon, the whole length of a façade. With the introduction of the Streamline Variant of the movement, portholes, prow-like projections, and poop-deckish articulations became popular. The Art Deco commercial building became a theatrical expression of business.

The style filtered down to even the most mundane and basic forms of architecture, particularly the public market. In the 1930s, planners and architects alike understood and utilized the power of Art Deco not only to enhance the community face through such symbols of style but also to impart, through architecture, the means of embracing progress even at the grassroots. The example of the public market

Banco Nacional de Filipinas, Iloilo Placer Branch, Plaza Libertad, Calle Real, Iloilo City, Province of Iloilo

Commercial banks traditionally adopt a particular architectural design for all their branches. The Banco Nacional de Filipinas, whose name was changed to Philippine National Bank, was no exception. This branch, built in the 1950s, shows the Egyptian theme of Art Deco, with massive, rounded piers supporting a truncated step pyramid-like top. The Egyptian look is also evident at the entrance with its pylon-like surround.

S. Villanueva Building,
Calle J.M. Basa corner Calle Arsenal,
Iloilo City, Province of Iloilo

Presumably designed and built in the 1930s, this lacelike filigree of a structure may have been the work of the master-architect Juan Arellano. It stands out among other Art Deco buildings in the city for its rich profusion of decorative reliefs—stylized foliage, rosettes, and geometric interplay.

Left. *Ramon Roces Building,*
Calle Soler, Quiapo, Manila

Designed by Pablo Antonio in the 1950s, it is a Streamline Moderne delight that once housed the Roces family's publishing and printing business, and later the Guzman Institute of Electronics. A play of vertical and horizontal elements, juxtaposed with clean, rounded forms, provides counterpoint and visual interest to the narrow access of Soler and Sales streets. Other Art Deco Streamline Moderne features are strategically located porthole windows and glass blocks. The building is being restored to its former glory.

Below. *Iloilo Public Market,*
Calle Rizal and Calle Gov. Caram
Iloilo City, Province of Iloilo

The City of Iloilo has a wealth of architectural legacies spanning almost two centuries, from Spanish colonial period Baroque or Revivalist architecture to Art Nouveaux of the first decades of the 20th century to a treasure chest of Art Deco buildings from the 1920s to the 1950s. One of its jewels is the public market built in the 1930s. Its main highlight is the towering entrance pylon at the corner capped with a modified lantern. The graceful tower, enhanced by vertical decorative elements as well as balcony-like projections, counterbalances the streamlined simplicity of its projecting flanks.

Jai Alai Building,
Taft Avenue, Manila

The Jai Alai Building in Manila was designed by Welton
Becket and built in 1939 for the Basque sport Pelota
which was loved by Filipinos. It was demolished in 2000.

Above left. *Bayview Hotel sticker, c. 1935.*

Above right. *Sunshine Bakery, Baguio City.*

Right. *Hotel City Lunch, Baguio City.*

Opposite page. *Postcard of the Rizal Memorial Tennis Stadium.*

as a theatrical and artistic venue did not escape the purveyors of Art Deco. The most significant example of an Art Deco public market is in Iloilo City.

The theatricality of the Art Deco movement as manifested in Philippine commercial architecture has made work not just a tedious task but an art as well. While lending itself to buildings that serve as venues for making and transacting money, the style has also given people engaged in the day-to-day struggle for survival an elevated sense of their worth. Sadly, this artistic expression is missing in most commercial buildings today. ☺

MANILA. PHILIPPINES

The Crystal Arcade

Gerard Rey Lico

The Crystal Arcade, inaugurated in June 1932, is the forerunner of our modern-day mall phenomenon. It places itself in architectural history as the most celebrated building of the early 20th century before it was completely destroyed in the last days of the Pacific War. Its name was derived from Joseph Paxton's London Crystal Palace (1851); both buildings share affinity with the remarkable use of glass as a major building component. Aside from being an excellent specimen of Art Deco style, it was the first shopping mall to introduce a walkway leading to the glass-walled shops on the first level.

Designed and partly owned by architect Andres Luna de San Pedro, the Crystal Arcade had an original plan that proposed a seven-story building with a ten-story central tower, but was partially completed as a three-story mall. The ₱1.5 million building used to stand on the Pardo de Tavera property, a lot that was accessible to both Escolta and San Vicente streets in Manila, a hub at that time of business and finance. Its site is now occupied by the Philippine National Bank.

Crystal Arcade was then considered the leading-edge structure in the country with its introduction of Art Deco's modernist strain, the Streamline Moderne, in the Philippine pre-war architectural milieu. Turning away from the exotic and excessive ornamentation of Art Deco's classical moderne (as can be seen in the Metropolitan Theater in Manila of Juan Arellano), the streamline Art Deco as the precursor of the international style valorized the sweeping horizontality of aerodynamic curves, flat roofs, glass blocks, banded windows, tubular steel railings, speed stripes, and mechanistically smooth wall surfaces and implied mass production. Stylistically, the Crystal Arcade supplemented the imagery used by industrial designers of airplanes, ocean liners, locomotives, automobiles, and household appliances. Its streamlining elements emphasized the futuristic projection of machine aesthetics and presented the archetype—a horizontal rectangular container with rounded corners or semi-circular bays, with smooth building skin, and surmounted by parapeted or projecting thin slab roof for the later commercial architecture which remained popular even in the 1950s.

Recovered photographs and plans have allowed us to reconstruct its make-up. The structure has a mezzanine at both sides of a central gallery that traverses the length of the gallery and is augmented at the center to culminate in a spacious lobby containing cantilevered winding staircases. The front and rear portions of the gallery are roofed by a simulated skylight made of polychromatic glass. A continuous strap of concrete walls and glass windows are conjoined to emphasize the building's horizontality. Art Deco bays are interrupted by a vertical window piercing both ends of the façade to counterbalance the tower at the central lobby. Each window storefront is of curved glass, while glass blocks are used at the mezzanine level. Ceramic tri-colored mosaic tiles adorn the floor in fan-shaped patterns. Colored Italian marble and granite facing provides the interior a sleek cosmopolitan flavor. Grillwork and stucco ornaments are marked by Art Deco motifs: diagonal lines, triangular geometric forms, and stylized foliage.

The symmetric building façade features continuous horizontal bands of concrete and windows that boldly curve inward as they converge over the central mall. The storefront level is rendered in a material of darker shade to make the upper bands appear visually light. Above the marquee-like canopy of the main entrance is a three-paneled stained-glass wall, bordered by a granite frame, and flanked by three other narrow vertical arrays of sculptural friezes to highlight the processional access.

After its construction, the building was foreclosed due to lack of tenants and the economic depression of the 1930s. In 1934, it served a new purpose when it housed the Manila Stock Exchange. In October 1936, the Crystal Arcade was sold to L.R. Nielson for ₱1.5 million. However, its eminence as the most highly regarded Filipino building of the 20th century was short-lived when Japanese Imperial forces tied bombs to its foundation before fleeing to Intramuros as the battle for Manila's liberation reached its final stretch in 1945. The atrocities of the war put an abrupt end to the glory that was the Crystal Arcade—and all the drama and beauty of the shopping experience it had stood for. ⑤

ART

and

Popcorn Palaces

Gerard Rey Lico

The origin of cinemas as a building form in the Philippines can be traced through the first exhibition of film in the country and the advent of electricity in the late 19th century. However, the predominance of the grandiose, stand-alone *sinehan* (movie house) as a new building typology coincided with the stylistic shift from Beaux Arts to Art Deco. It was created by a burgeoning film industry that enabled the public to see films *en masse*.

Lyric Theater, Escolta, Manila

Your Guarantee to Higher Entertainment

The "GRAND" THEATRE

The "STATE" THEATRE

The "AVENUE" THEATRE

**ALL LOCATED IN
THE DOWNTOWN SECTION
OF RIZAL AVENUE**

Detail of an advertisement for theaters located in the downtown section of Rizal Avenue, Manila.

The cinema palaces of the Art Deco period were thus not only a unique architectural genre devoted to watching movies, but also an exercise in extravagance and ostentatious grandeur that drew Filipinos to the quasi-religious allure of Hollywood. The promise of aesthetic stimulation and glamour within dimly lit interiors rivalled the numinous ecclesiastical architecture of the previous colonial era, facilitating the slow but effective acculturation of the native subjects to the American way of life as they swooned at the altar of projected images and deco decadence.

Architecturally, the *sinehan* was merely a box with a decorated façade. Theater owners then realized that whimsical architecture sold tickets and gave their establishments a unique identity, which the exotic motifs of the Art Deco stylistic menu readily supplied.

The attraction of film-going was based not only on the movie that one went to see, but also on the total architectural environment which allowed audiences to spend time in a place detached from the harsh and dull surroundings of quotidian life. Once people entered the theater, they would pass through a series of spaces: entrance vestibule, foyers, lobbies, lounges, upper-level promenade, and waiting rooms. Among those spaces, the lobby—with its many distractions such as stained-glass, relief sculptures, ornate fountains and statuary—would most stimulate the flights of fancy of a large crowd.

Three National Artists figured in the making of this mural for Capitol Theater in Escolta, Manila—Carlos Francisco (extreme left), Architect Juan Nakpil (extreme right) and, beside him, Victorio Edades. Flanking the left sculpture are Severino Fabie and Galo Ocampo.

The introduction of sound on August 2, 1929, via RKO's *Pennsylvanian Syncopation* at Radio Theater, a renovated theater formerly known as the Majestic at Plaza Santa Cruz, Manila, had a major impact on the design of cinemas. It eliminated the need for an orchestra pit and full stage facilities for live accompaniment and live show intermissions. The pulsating façades of the new cinemas were also an expression of sound. Radio Theater demonstrated this tendency with a soaring ziggurat-like façade embellished by bas-relief of cubistic human figures constituting a jazz quartet whose propulsive rhythm was expressed through a series of concentric circles penetrated by sharp and stylized thunderbolts and waveforms.

Above. *Radio Theater, Plaza Santa Cruz, Manila*

Right. *State Theater, Rizal Avenue, Manila*

There was another expression of Art Deco's opulence in movie theaters—the locally derived and familiar vernacular designs. Juan Arellano's Metropolitan Theater in Manila had Philippine floral motifs, bamboo banister railings, carved banana and mango ceiling reliefs, and batik mosaic patterns. Philippine fauna, such as the carabao head, figured prominently on the façade of Juan Nakpil's State Theater (1935) in Rizal Avenue, Manila. Fernando Ocampo's Pines Theater (1939) in Baguio was suffused with Igorot design patterns. Human figures garbed in native costumes, such as those on the elevations of Nakpil's Capitol Theater (1935) in Escolta, Manila, also reflected this leaning towards the indigenous. Capitol's original interior made use of the national flower, the *sampaguita* (jasmine), as central motif on the wrought-iron grills on the stairs, the lobby, the foyer, and the proscenium arch.

This page. *Pines Theater, Baguio City.*

This page and opposite. *Capitol Theater, Escolta, Manila*

Above. *Times Theater, Quezon Boulevard, Quiapo, Manila.*

Opposite page. *Life Theater, Quezon Boulevard, Quiapo, Manila.*

From the 1930s to the 1940s, the design of cinemas gave way to smooth curves with an aura of precision and the exactitudes of the power of the machine. Designers responded to the economic constraints of the time by eliminating from the structure the profusion of applied ornament in favor of a more austere variant of Art Deco known as Streamlined Moderne. Inspired in part by great transatlantic ocean liners, the new style featured aerodynamic curves, smooth wall surfaces, and steel railings often marked by the signature trio of horizontal speed stripes that were meant to suggest motion. Pablo Antonio's Ideal Theater (1933) on Rizal Avenue, Manila and Lyric Theater (1937) in Escolta, Manila and Luis Araneta's Times Theater (1941) on Quezon Boulevard, Quiapo, Manila, exemplify this step into architectural austerity. The entrance to the Ideal was flanked by two massive pillars between vertical bands. Besides the Pines and Session theaters in Baguio, other cinema houses in the Art Deco style were built outside Manila, like the Oriente in Cebu. The white façade of Life Theater fused Art Deco streaming and neoclassicism with its exaggeratedly scaled round columns tipped with conical finials.

27 Rizal Ave., Manila.

Opposite and this page. *Ideal Theater, Rizal Avenue, Manila*

The tourist guidebook *Manila and the Philippines*, published in 1933 by the American Express Company, listed twenty movie houses. Only two of them survive today: the decrepit Metropolitan Theater (1931) on Padre Burgos Avenue, Manila, and the last fully functional single-screen theater, the Cine Bellevue (1933) in Paco, Manila, which had an Orientalist leitmotif that employed the Neo-Mudejar Art Deco strain and has been converted into a clothing store. The so-called popcorn palaces have succumbed to the call of the times. The once-glorious architectural tribute to the world of extravagant imagination has faded to black. ◎

Below. *Metropolitan Theater, Padre Burgos Avenue, Manila*

Opposite page. *Metropolitan Theater auditorium.*

No. 7   METROPOLITAN THEATRE, MANILA.

Contributing Authors'
PROFILES

Gerard Rey Lico

Gerard Rey Lico is an architect and art historian. He graduated from a BS in Architecture in 1997, an MA in Art History in 2000, and a Ph.D. in 2007. He teaches at the University of the Philippines (UP) College of Fine Arts and practices architecture as the Campus Architect of the same institution.

He is the author of *Edifice Complex: Power, Myth and Marcos State Architecture* (2003), the video series *Audio-Visual Textbook of Philippine Architecture* (2007), *Arkitekturang Filipino: A History of Architecture and Urbanism in the Philippines* (2008) and a series of interactive cd-roms such as *Arkitekturang Filipino: Spaces and Places in History* (2003), *Through the Lens of an American Soldier* (2004), and *Building Modernity: A Century of Philippine Architecture and Allied Arts* (2008).

For his research work in architectural history and cultural studies, he was conferred the UP *Gawad Chanselor para sa Pinakamahusay na Mananaliksik* (Arts and Humanities) in the years 2002, 2004 and 2005, installing him to its Hall of Fame. He was one of the recipients of the Ten Outstanding Young Men (TOYM) in 2004 and conferred as a University Artist of the UP in 2009.

Apart from his academic and professional practice, he currently holds office as the Vice Head of the National Committee on Architecture and Allied of the National Commission for Culture and the Arts, the Research Program Director of the University of the Philippines' College of Fine Arts, the Curator of the Museum of Filipino Architecture at the University of the Philippines and the Executive Director of the Centre for Filipino Architecture of the United Architects of the Philippines.

Lourdes R. Montinola

Lourdes Reyes Montinola's main interests lie in the field of art and culture, education, and lately in heritage conservation. While chair of the board of trustees of the Far Eastern University, and board member of other affiliate corporations and foundations, she is a member of the Oriental Ceramic Society, the Museum Foundation of the Philippines, the Heritage Conservation Society, the Asia Society Philippine Foundation, the English Speaking Union (Philippines) Inc., and the Philippine Textile Society.

Her definitive work on pineapple cloth, *Piña* (1991), was written because of a desire to preserve a national treasure in danger of extinction. It won the Manila Critics' Circle National Book Award for Art and helped revive the *piña*-weaving industry. *Breaking the Silence* (1996) won the Manila Critics' Circle Award for Biography. It was also selected by the Editorial Board as a University of the Philippines Press Centennial Publication in 2008. She has contributed to other award-winning anthologies and publications.

Mrs. Montinola holds a Bachelor of Arts degree from Marymount College in New York, an MA in Cultural History from the Asean Graduate Institute of Arts. She completed the Management Development Program for College and University Administrators in the Institute for Educational Management, Graduate School of Education, Harvard University, and she obtained her Ph.D. in English: Creative Writing from the University of the Philippines.

Among her awards, she received the Outstanding Manilan Award in the field of Education and Administration, on the occasion of the 433rd Araw ng Maynila on June 23, 2004.

She served as Head of the Cultural Committee and Member of the Board of Directors of the Alliance Française de Manille (1987-1989) and as President in 1989-1991. She was conferred the decoration for Officier des Arts et des Lettres by the Republic of France and the Alliance Française de Manille on July 9, 2008.

Manuel Maximo Lopez del Castillo-Noche

Manuel Maximo Lopez del Castillo-Noche, an architect by profession, is currently Assistant Professor Level III at the College of Architecture, University of Santo Tomas (UST), and Senior Researcher of the Research Cluster for Culture, Education, and Social Issues, also of the UST.

With the Research Cluster for Culture, Education and Social Issues, he has undertaken researches centering on Spanish Colonial Architecture and Engineering. He has recently received six grants from the Program for Cultural Cooperation, The Ministry of Education, Culture and Sports, Kingdom of Spain for his work on the Spanish Colonial Lighthouses in the Philippines, entitled *Lonely Sentinels of the Sea: The Spanish Colonial Lighthouses in the Philippines,* amongst others. Also with the Research Cluster for Culture, Education and Social

Issues, Professor Noche has undertaken researches on built heritage such as colonial baptisteries and cemeteries, church retablos, and Spanish era bridges.

Professor Noche in his capacity as an architect and a historian also writes articles focusing on built colonial heritage. He has written two books on colonial architecture and infrastructure and was a regular contributor to *Design and Architecture Magazine* from 1998 onwards. He more recently contributes to the *Philippine Daily Inquirer*, *Pilmap Travel and Leisure*, *BluPrint Magazine* and the College of Architectures' *Vision Magazine*. Architect Noche's interest in colonial architecture similarly has made him familiar with the plight of these legacies of the past, having documented substantially the remains of these legacies: i.e., churches, cemeteries, lighthouses, bridges, train stations, and more recently the colonial retables of churches.

Professor Noche has an MS in Architecture majoring in Environmental Design and Engineering from the Bartlett School of Architecture and Planning, University College, London, UK, and a Bachelors in Science degree from the College of Architecture and Fine Arts, University of Santo Tomas.

John L. Silva

John L. Silva is an author and has written pieces concerning photography, Philippine history, and the arts. Mr. Silva is a collector of rare Philippine books and 19th century photographs. He has curated exhibitions on Philippine photographic history in the United States and the Philippines, and was Senior Consultant for the National Museum. Currently, he sits on the board of the Mangyan Heritage Society, Synergeia Foundation, Hands On Manila, Ballet Philippines and the Manila Symphony Orchestra.

He teaches arts appreciation to public school teachers and is the author of *Loving the Arts*, a teachers workbook.

He is currently writing a photography book on studio photography in the 1930's.

He graduated with a Masters Degree in Philippine American History at Goddard College in Vermont, United States.

Born in Iloilo City, he lived as a child in the Ledesma Boathouse along with his sister Marie. His interest in Art Deco was initiated by living as a child in one such unique house in the Philippines.

Augusto F. Villalón

Mr. Villalón is an architect and cultural heritage planner based in Manila. He received a Ph.D. in Humanities (Honoris Causa), Far Eastern University, Manila; Master of Architecture, Yale University; BA Sociology/History of Art, University of Notre Dame.

Awards received include the UNESCO Asia-Pacific Cultural Heritage Award in 2003 and 2005 for architectural heritage conservation projects in Manila; *Gintong Karangalan* Professional Achievement Award from the United Architects of the Philippines; La Sallian Achievement Award and the Scholarum Award, both from De La Salle University, Manila; Exemplary Alumnus Award, University of Notre Dame; Lifetime Achievement Award for Heritage Conservation, National Commission for Culture and the Arts (NCCA); United Architects of the Philippines, elevation to College of Fellows; *Patnubay ng Sining at Kalinangan*, Medallion of Honor from the City of Manila; and the Padre Burgos Award from the City of Vigan.

His firm A Villalón Architects is involved in architecture, real estate development, and cultural heritage planning including conservation, community development and cultural tourism. Aside from professional work in the Philippines, his firm undertakes international consultancies for private entities, foreign governments, and international agencies such as UNESCO, ITC-UNCTAD/GATT, UNIDO, UN-World Tourism Organization, and the International Council for Monuments and Sites (ICOMOS) where he was a Member of its Executive Committee until 2005. Mr. Villalón now serves as a Member of the ICOMOS International Advisory Committee and is currently President of its Philippine Committee. He is also an adviser of the World Monuments Fund in New York City.

He was a Member of the UNESCO National Commission of the Philippines, serving as the Philippine representative to the UNESCO World Heritage Committee in Paris from 1989-2001.

He also served on the Board of Commissioners of the NCCA, the de facto Ministry of Culture of the Philippines, having headed the NCCA Subcommission for Cultural Heritage and the NCCA Committee on Monuments and Sites.

Completed Philippine projects include the preparation of World Heritage Nomination Dossiers for all five Philippine sites inscribed in the World Heritage List: Tubbataha Reef, the Baroque Churches of the Philippines, Rice Terraces of the Philippine Cordilleras, Historic City of Vigan, Puerto Princesa Subterranean River National Park. Architectural conservation projects include the Gota de Leche and Far Eastern University in Manila, both recipients of the UNESCO Asia-Pacific Cultural Heritage Award. His firm also has completed heritage master planning for the campuses of Philippine Women's University and De La Salle University, both in Manila.

Other completed work includes conservation and cultural tourism planning for historic settlements in Sichuan and Shandong provinces (China), and for Buddhist pilgrimage sites in southern Nepal. He has prepared Heritage Impact Assessments for new developments within World Heritage areas in the Rice Terraces of the

Philippine Cordilleras, the World Heritage Cities of George Town and Malacca (Malaysia), and participated as a Keynote Speaker and technical expert in the Organization of World Heritage Cities Congress in Quito, Ecuador.

Living Landscapes and Cultural Landmarks—World Heritage Sites in the Philippines, published by ArtPostAsia and supported by the World Heritage Center, was launched in 2007 at UNESCO Headquarters in Paris. He authored *Lugar*, which won the National Book Award and the Alfonso Ongpin Award for Best Art Book in 2002. In 2001, the Ministerio de Asuntos Exteriores in Madrid published his book, *Manila*. Other studies, articles and academic papers have been published internationally or presented in meetings and fora. He is a heritage columnist in the *Philippine Daily Inquirer*.

Stylized railing with the letters FEU at the Far Eastern University, Manila.

ACKNOWLEDGMENTS

by the editor

We wish to thank the following Art Deco lovers without whom this publication would not have been possible. Thank you for believing in the importance of Art Deco in the Philippines and helping make people aware of the need to conserve our heritage and whatever remains of this beautiful style.

First and foremost, Rev. Rodrigo Perez, OSB, Benedictine monk and architect who first invited a group of friends and me to view Art Deco landmark buildings north of the Pasig River "before they disappear". To our surprise, the first building we visited was the Main Building of the Far Eastern University (FEU).

Pablo Antonio Jr. and his children who helped FEU restore its heritage buildings, especially after a fire and an earthquake. Also Ramon Antonio who remodeled the parts of the Main Building after the fire.

Augusto (Toti) F. Villalón who inspired us with his appreciation of the FEU buildings and campus to continue restoring them properly, thus earning for the university a UNESCO Asia-Pacific Cultural Heritage Award in 2005.

Eulalia (Laling) Lim, daughter of Gen. and Mrs. Vicente Lim who provided us a first close look at an Art Deco house, Philippine style—her parents' residence at Vito Cruz, now P. Ocampo.

Roberto Lim and family, especially Gina, Laida, and Miko Lim, who allowed us to study and document the magnificent Tomas Mapua house. Josephine Labrador Hermano, publisher of Design and Architecture Magazine, *which served as a reference and photo source for the Mapua house.*

The other Vito Cruz residents—Regina Roces Paterno, granddaughter of Justice Antonio Villareal, for allowing us to feature her ancestral home, now converted into a boutique hotel; Inday Lacson Gabaldon and Ditas Javellana Jalbuena, who provided us information regarding their parents' homes; Mr. Federico Montinola and family, who kindly allowed us to photograph their lovely home.

The Government Service Insurance System, which owns the Metropolitan Theater in Manila, for its interest in this project. President and General Manager Robert G. Vergara and Ms. Margie Jorillo, for their kind support.

Mayor Alfredo Lim and Gemma Cruz Araneta for their great interest and support in the restoration of the Metropolitan Theater and for facilitating our visit for a photo session. The National Commission for Culture and the Arts (NCCA) for their efforts in the revival of the theater as well. NCCA Chairman Vilma L. Labrador, Executive Director Malou Jacob, and former NCAA Director Cecile Guidote-Alvarez for their assistance in this project.

Gerard Rey Lico of the University of the Philippines for facilitating and providing additional archival photos. Writer and artist Alfredo Roces who gave a vintage photo of the Ideal Theater.

Gianna Montinola for her help in marketing and publicity. Josie Azupardo and Ma. Cristina Talampas for their secretarial help.

We thank all those art lovers who encouraged us in our quest for Art Deco examples in architecture: the late Zafiro Ledesma in Iloilo who opened the museum of Iloilo and his beautiful home to us and encouraged us to pursue our study of Art Deco; Fernando (Pandot) Ocampo Jr., son of Fernando Ocampo who built the Don Eugenio Lopez boathouse in Iloilo, for providing us with information about the house which he restored; the late Congressman Bienvenido O. Marquez and Mrs. Erlinda O. Marquez for allowing us to feature their home in Sariaya, Quezon; Jose Ma. Ricardo Panlilio of the Dasmariñas Museum, who shared his vast knowledge of beautiful Sariaya homes.

To the countless people we interviewed and who generously gave us information, to the people who allowed us to use their photographs: Cedie Lopez-Vargas of the Lopez Museum, Tina Turralba, Benjie Toda, Sylvia Roces Montilla, and Zymon Bumatay, FEU photographer.

Opposite page. *Far Eastern University chapel exterior with a specially made tile mural of Our Lady of Fatima by Vicente Manansala.*

PHOTO CREDITS

Zymon Bumatay
1, 2, 4, 5, 10, 14, 28, 29, 30, 31, 57, 59, 60, 61, 62, 63, 64, 65, 66, 67, 68, 69 (bottom), 70, 71, 72, 73, 74, 75, 76, 77, 78, 79, 80, 81, 84 (top), 91 (top), 92, 93, 94, 95, 100 (bottom, rightmost), 102, 133, 136

Miko Lim
5, 15, 35, 38 (bottom), 39, 40, 41, 42, 43, 144

Melvin Patawaran
51, 52, 53, 54

Benjie Toda
11, 36-37 (with permission from Design and Architecture Magazine)

Tina Turralba
47

FROM THE COLLECTION OF:

Gerard Rey Lico
82, 90 (top right), 114, 115, 116, 117, 118, 119, 120, 121, 122, 123, 124, 125, 127, 128

Roberto and Gloria (Mapua) Lim
6, 16, 32, 34, 38 (top)

Lourdes R. Montinola
cover, 9, 12, 13, 17, 18, 19, 20, 21, 22, 23, 24, 27 (bottom), 56, 58, 69 (top), 83, 84 (bottom), 84-85, 86, 87, 89, 90 (top left, bottom), 91 (bottom), 96, 97, 98, 99, 100 (top; bottom, leftmost and middle), 101, 103, 129, 137

Francisco J. Nakpil
25, 26

Manuel Maximo Lopez del Castillo-Noche
104, 105, 106, 107, 108, 109, 110

Jose Ma. Ricardo Panlilio
50

Regina Roces Paterno
27 (top)

Alfredo Roces
126

John L. Silva
44, 45, 46, 48, 49, 111, 112, 113

DISCLAIMER: All efforts were exhausted to credit the photographs in this book. Photographs on a page are from the same source unless otherwise indicated.

Opposite page. *Bas-relief depicting Modern Times at the Far Eastern University Administration Building, Manila by Francesco Riccardo Monti.*

This page. *Detail on exterior of the Metropolitan Theater.*

INDEX

Above. *A bas-relief from the interior wall of the Metropolitan Theater, Manila*

Page 144. *Detail on buffet table door from the dining room of the Tomas Mapua house on Taft Avenue Extension, Pasay City.*